ON TIME'S PASSAGE

ON TIME & PLACE

Other Works by Sandy Krolick

Вероника: Сибирская Сказка (Novel)
Veronika: The Siberian's Tale (Novel)
The Recovery of Ecstasy: Notebooks from Siberia
Apocalypse of Barbarians: Inquisitions on Empire
Conversations On A Country Path
Gandhi in the Postmodern Age
Recollective Resolve
Ethical Decision-making Styles
Культурный критицизм
Myth, Mystery and Magic: Religion in Ancient Egypt
Russian Soul and Collapse of the West
Shambhala (Novel)
Misha (Novel)
On Being and Being Good
Q: Interpreting QAnon
A New Heaven and a New Earth
Philosophic Play
Babel Unhinged
The Siberian Shaman and Western Myth
Notebooks: Philosophical Memoirs
Expelled From The Garden
Agnosis and Parousia
The Strange Case of Donald Trump

Other Works by Sandy Krolick

ON TIME'S PASSAGE

SANDY KROLICK, PH.D.

ISLANDS PRESS

NEW YORK : ALTAI KRAI : FLORIDA

ISBN: 979-8-9919579-0-8

Cover art courtesy of
Yuri Ivanov
Altai Krai, Russia

*Profundity of thought belongs to youth,
clarity of thought to old age.*

Friedrich Nietzsche, *Human, All Too Human*

On Time's Passage

As we reluctantly and incredulously grow older, time seems to slip by ever more quickly, much like an express train running through its regularly scheduled stops with an invisible conductor's eye closely glued to his pocket-watch, just counting down the remaining minutes of his trip. Of course, it is both normal and natural to focus on the affairs of everyday life when we are young, and the temporal flow is not really at issue, where every event is simply another notch in the belt or milestone reached. But there appears to be a certain moment in time when the *end* definitely feels much closer than the *beginning*. And while the sense of an ending will vary from one person to the next, its weightiness cannot be ignored, the urgency of its approach, unmistakable.

For those who are philosophically inclined it seems only natural, if daunting, to reflect on the overall course of one's life, recalling those eddies and diversions experienced along the way. But it is, more often than not, the smallest fissures in this temporal flow that somehow rise up from our unconscious when we least expect them, challenging our very capacity to move forward without first hesitating on some pleasant or unpleasant bit of memory that emerges from the depths. As disjointed as these memories may appear, such apparitions serve as exclamation points on life's frailty, reminders of the distance traveled over the entirety of our personal histories. But if time itself is at issue, we must reflect on the meaning of it's passage, including why time often seems to slow to a crawl while alternatively speeding up like a bullet train. Why this variability in our perception of temporal flow?

Attempting to loosen the chains binding us to its apparently unyielding forward march, while allowing us to get behind this common place view of time's passage, I will recall some remarks by the late philosopher, Maurice Merleau-Ponty.

> *We say that time passes or flows by. We speak of the course of time... If time is similar to a river, it flows from the past toward the present and the future... But this often repeated metaphor is in reality extremely confused... [In fact] the volume of water already carried by is not moving towards the future, but sinking into the past; what is to come is on the side of the source, for time does not come from the past. It is not the past that pushes the present, nor the present that pushes the future, into being; the future is not prepared behind the observer, it is a brooding presence moving to meet him, like a*

storm on the horizon. If the observer sits in a boat and is carried by the current, we may say that he is moving downstream towards his future, but the future lies in the new landscapes which await him at the estuary, and the course of time is no longer the stream itself, but the landscape as it rolls by for the moving observer. (1)

Suffice it to say that the future is *always already* approaching, both figuratively and literally, as our past vanishes in the wake of new vistas and experiences. But why does our sense of time's course feel so capricious, sometimes seeming to pass more quickly while at other times apparently dragging on so slowly? What is it about our lived-experience that creates such divergent impressions of time's passage? And what role does memory or recollection play in our perception of this temporal flow? Finally, then, what grounds that taken-for-granted scaffolding upon which hangs all of human history and personal autobiography?

Undeniably, there are challenges raised with the emergence of historical consciousness. Chief among them is a vague apprehension driving us inexorably forward along with the sense that life's purpose is in some way tied to this forward temporal flow. But what has such a fixation on the future – having been drilled into us since youth – done for us or to us? Has it not created a disquieting sense of abandonment as we continue to pursue this never-ending quest for self-fulfillment? Has it not prompted a vague feeling of emptiness from which we cannot easily recover, and as protection against which we need the distraction of more planning with ever more refined goals and objectives? Is not the net result of this temporal mandate a *de facto* emptying of the present moment, an erasure of the significance of immediate experience, except perhaps as a stepping-stone to some final reckoning that inevitably ends in death? How, then, do we break this spell of historical consciousness or the idea of the unidirectional flow of time that has been cast like a pall over humanity for more than six millennia?

Again we turn briefly to Merleau-Ponty work where he writes about "...the thickness of the pre-objective present, in which we find our bodily being, our social being, and the pre-existence of the world..."(2) His words here serve as a stark reminder that there is something forgotten or hidden within the *density* of the present moment; there is an *opacity* underlying our culturally-framed experience of time's passage — something linking us to the earth, enlivening our sense of presence — something felt as more *primal* than those theories or hypotheses of modern science.

In light of the above, it would seem that the principal issue facing us is the challenge – indeed the illusion – of unidirectional time itself, and the extent to which this misapprehension of forward temporal flow helps constitute our sense of self, of life's purpose, and finally, our sense of an ending. As the cultural historian, Marvin Bram, reminds us:

> *The selfsame future in which we plan our next and better job, or arrange for a wedding or for college, is the only site on the temporal scheme past/ present/future in which we will cease to live. We die in the future. Here is a hypothesis: the more absorbed with planning a person is, the more likely that fear of death will become a continuous presence for that person.*(3)

Of course, the cultural toolkit we acquired during early childhood socialization sought to focus us exclusively on this unfolding chronological trajectory, relentlessly moving us forward from past to future, with an overriding emphasis on making progress and 'making something of yourself'. Yet there are unmistakable signs that our remotest ancestor, *Homo Erectus*, living some two million years ago during the Pleistocene Epoch, had little if any appetite for this idea of unidirectional time or, for that matter, any sense of historical progress. Rather, these early *hominins* were immersed in a uniquely ahistorical niche where the present moment was continuously reconstituted in conjunction with regular periodicities — the solar, lunar, and vegetative cycles of death, rebirth and renewal. For primal humanity, then, life was lived in a moment that remained in closest proximity to the cycles and rhythms of nature.

In fact, some of the earliest traces of human culture in primitive art and myth suggest that early representatives of our own species, *Homo Sapiens,* affirmed their kinship with the same natural cycles and periodicities. It has even been suggested by various scholars that these primal forebears knew nothing of the 'burden of history' that would later come to characterize civilized consciousness. And, it is back there, at the origins of our species, that we might again find guidance in reframing the emotional and physical challenges of time's apparent forward march, and help us better come to terms with the natural processes of aging and death. We might find there a perspective on life — not as a simple linear progression with a fixed termination point — but rather, as part of that natural periodicity, including those key elements of rebirth and renewal.

In closing, let us briefly reconsider memory or recollection in relation to life's natural periodicity. The term 'recollection' derives from the Latin root, *colligere*, meaning 'to gather or collect', while the prefix, *re,* means 'again'. Given this etymology we might say the experiences that helped shape our lives — having become hidden from consciousness — suddenly return, erupting onto the scene, only to be re-cognized or 'known again'. Memories, as remnants of such lived-experience, seem to be stored within the very bones, muscles, and folds of our flesh, helping constitute the very thickness of life itself. We might say, there's an unconscious repository of experience that helps craft who we have become today. In this respect, memories act much like those repetitions found within nature itself, e.g., the waxing and waning of the moon, or the rising and setting of the sun — serving to remind us of the periodicity of life and our own lived-experience. Embracing such memories might help us face the uncertainty of a future that is *always, already* coming to meet us, while enabling us to accept the inevitability of death as well.

> *Let go! Float on the Great Transformation, with neither joy nor fear. When it's all over, it's over. Brooding Serves no purpose.* (4)

Text Notes

1. Maurice Merleau-Ponty, *Phenomenology of Perception*, 1976, pp. 411-412

2. Ibid, p. 433

3. Sandy Krolick, *Recovery of Ecstasy*, p. ix

4. From 'Substance, Shadow, and Spirit,' a poem by Tao Yuanming, Chinese poet living during the Eastern Jin and Liu Song Dynasties (365-427).

www.ingramcontent.com/pod-product-compliance
Lightning Source LLC
Chambersburg PA
CBHW071348290326
41933CB00041B/3147